Tools for Healing

Simple, Creative Ways to Explore, Learn From,
and Resolve Emotional Distress

Tools
for Healing

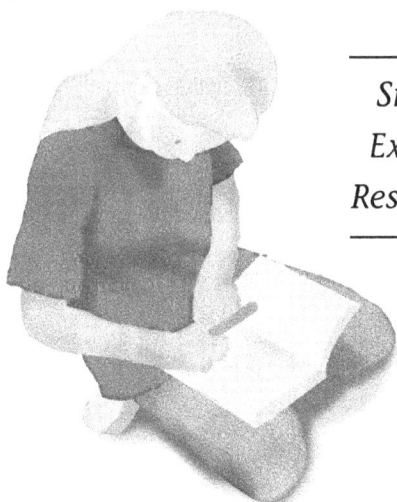

Simple, Creative Ways to
Explore, Learn From, and
Resolve Emotional Distress

Kira Freed

Two Hawks Press
Tucson, AZ

To the Findhorn Foundation with gratitude
for countless contributions to my inner life

and

to Charlie
for honoring my inner life
and trusting me with yours

Tools for Healing: Simple, Creative Ways to Explore,
Learn From, and Resolve Emotional Distress

This book recommends activities for wellness but is by no means
a substitute for medical or psychiatric care.

Quotation on page 3 used with permission from Deborah
Daw Heffernan. Exercise on pages 14 and 15 adapted with permission
from Piero Ferrucci. All reasonable efforts have been made to contact
the author of the quotations on pages 1 and 5.

Cover art and author photo by Charlie Alolkoy

Two Hawks Press
www.twohawkspress.com

ISBN: 978-0-9967305-2-5

Printed in the United States of America

Table of Contents

Note to the Reader

The content of this book is included in my memoir about the remarkable transformations I went through in the process of grieving my father's death and healing from the effects of an abusive childhood. In that book, I share many of my own experiences of using these tools as well as including them as an appendix. After the book was published, a friend suggested that I make the appendix available as a stand-alone book. I liked the idea. (Thanks, Mark!)

If you're interested in learning more about these tools and/or about healing from grief or childhood abuse, please check out my memoir:

Losing and Finding My Father
Seasons of Grief, Healing and Forgiveness

by Kira Freed

Foreword by Richard C. Schwartz,
developer of the Internal Family Systems
model of psychotherapy

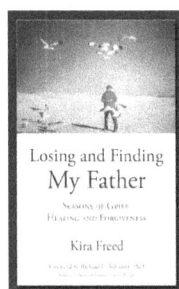

Available in print and ebook editions
through Amazon, Barnes & Noble, Apple, and Kobo

INTRODUCTION

The tools in this book are offered much like a platter of hors d'oeuvres to give you a taste of several kinds of inner work. They are not intended as a comprehensive treatment of each of the topics. The recommended resources section at the back of the book lists many avenues for investigating these tools in greater depth.

If you are new to this kind of work, give yourself time to acclimate to the adventure of self-exploration. Some people take to it right away, while others learn to access their inner world more gradually. Like most everything in life, it gets easier with practice. Be gentle with yourself and honor your own pace.

The tools included in this book—active imagination, art, journaling, and working with the observer self and subpersonalities— are rich ways to work with the unconscious, a part of our mind that contains material of which we are mostly unaware in everyday life. In the words of Jungian analyst Robert A. Johnson,

> *The unconscious is a marvelous universe of unseen energies, forces, forms of intelligence—even distinct personalities—that live within us. It is a much larger realm than most of us realize, one that has a complete life of its own running parallel to the ordinary life we live day to day. The unconscious is the secret source of much of our thought, feeling, and behavior. It influences us in ways that are all the more powerful because unsuspected.* (*Inner Work*, p. 3)

While the unconscious is by definition not conscious, the parts closest to consciousness and most ready to come into awareness can be accessed and engaged with a good dose of intention and the assistance of various tools. I think of this process as the leading edge of our individual healing.

The native language of the unconscious is the language of symbols. By accessing these symbols and bringing them to consciousness, we can work with their energies and develop a relationship with them. Working with our inner symbols can strengthen the connection between conscious and unconscious aspects of self, providing for increasingly open communication between the two as well as strengthening intuitive abilities.

You might have an intuition to talk with an imaginary giant orange parrot, to draw a secret underground world, to write a letter to a grandparent you never met, or to acknowledge a needy child part of yourself. The trick is to follow through on the intuition without first trying to make sense of it—in other words, to trust that the intuition is worth exploring without first filtering it through the rational mind.

The tools in this book can facilitate the expression of intuitive promptings in safe ways and in a safe setting. This doesn't mean you'll go out into the world in an uncensored way; it means you'll learn how to explore deeper levels of yourself in private. This work can help you integrate unconscious, or shadow, aspects of yourself that you may currently be expressing in ways that do not serve your well-being (such as addictions, dysfunctional relationships, self-sabotage, illness, and more). This work can also contribute to global healing, as is eloquently expressed in this quote by Deborah Daw Heffernan:

I have always believed that each and every one of us is responsible for doing her own emotional homework, for doing the best we can with our gifts and constraints. The process of facing down our ghosts is our small, attainable contribution to a kinetic process that holds the potential for healing the world. And why not? After all, the opposite is true: history has proven that people who are unwilling to catch and release their individual sadnesses, disappointments, and hidden motivations have compensated by wreaking havoc on the world. Good and evil lie within each of us, and every day we choose which potential to fill.

(*An Arrow Through the Heart*, p. 190)

ACTIVE IMAGINATION

In the book *Inner Work*, Robert Johnson delineates two ways of working with symbols in the unconscious—active imagination and dreamwork. Active imagination accesses these symbols in a waking state, while dreamwork accesses them during sleep. (I do not include dreamwork in this book because I lack sufficient background to present the topic. However, dreamwork can be a rich tool for doing inner work, and many books, including Johnson's, exist for those interested in working with their dreams.)

Active imagination, a process developed by Carl Jung, refers to various means of exploring unconscious material through the use of creative fantasy, giving voice to images and symbols in the unconscious. Active imagination involves bringing the images to consciousness and engaging with them through the use of dialogue. The dialogue can be spoken, written, drawn, danced, or anything else you can think of. (I focus on spoken and written dialogue in this section; see the section on art therapy for a discussion of art and other nonverbal modes of expression.) The "Conversations with My Father" chapter of my memoir, *Losing and Finding My Father*, is an example of dialogues that were spoken aloud, recorded, and later transcribed. I have also conversed with images in complete silence. There are no rules—it's about discovering what works best for you and takes you to a place where you can effectively engage with the images and discover their messages.

A good skill to cultivate in doing active imagination and other inner work is the ability to do what I call "catching the tail" of buried thoughts and feelings by noticing and allowing into awareness the first thing that comes to your mind. "Catching the tail" helps bring forth symbols hovering on the fence between unconsciousness and consciousness. To develop the skill of "catching the tail," pay attention to whatever comes into your awareness if someone asks what you're feeling or what your preference is in a given situation. If your first instinct is to deny the feeling or quash the impulse to voice your own desires, it's a clue that the "tail" you're trying to catch is buried. Affirm your wish to become aware of your feelings and desires, and keep practicing. Welcoming your authentic responses makes more space for them in your life.

Active imagination isn't simply a mental exercise—it's also an energetic and emotional engagement with our images and symbols. In Johnson's words:

> *This experience, to be sure, is symbolic. The images with whom we interact are symbols, and we encounter them on a symbolic plane of existence. But a magical principle is at work: When we experience the images, we also directly experience the inner parts of ourselves that are clothed in the images. This is the power of symbolic experience in the human psyche when it is entered into consciously: Its intensity and its effect on us is often as concrete as a physical experience would be. Its power to realign our attitudes, teach us and change us at deep levels, is much greater than that of external events that we may pass through without noticing. (Inner Work, p. 25)*

Johnson provides a note of caution, repeated here, to people new to active imagination. It's important to have access to someone who can help you in the event that you feel overwhelmed by the imagination or can't cut it off when you want to. To newcomers, the images may at times feel powerful enough to overtake your personality, and the emotions you access may feel too strong or vivid. Be sure you have someone to call on for help and grounding as needed until you become familiar with the process.

Feeling overwhelmed is rarely a problem, however, and in fact the opposite is generally true—people often have more difficulty immersing themselves in their imagination than separating themselves from it. However, until you know how you will respond, it's best to have a safety net.

Keep in mind that opening a door to your inner world rarely happens in one sitting. If you're accustomed to pushing away that world in your everyday life, it's not going to magically appear full-blown the first time you open the door. Much like a person who's been dismissed repeatedly, your inner awareness is likely to doubt your sincerity the first few times you invite it to reveal itself. Demonstrate your good intentions by extending the invitation repeatedly instead of giving up if you don't have a cosmic experience the first time.

You can also demonstrate your good intentions by being willing to take what comes. You might hope for a fairy godmother dressed in powder blue and a halo who will offer you clear, loving, and inspired guidance. If you instead get a giant alligator with razor-sharp teeth and wicked-looking eyes (as once happened to me), try to stay with the process and hear what it has to say. And remember that you get to have a voice, too. If you're afraid of the alligator, tell it. If you want it to move back twenty feet, say so and then make it happen. Find a balance between honoring your need for safety and your desire to step outside your comfort zone in order to cultivate a relationship with your unconscious. If the alligator showed up, you can trust that something rich and valuable can emerge from dialoguing with it.

Try This: Invite Images Through Active Imagination
- Find a quiet space and time away from your everyday routine. Arrange to be free of interruption by family members, pets, and the telephone. Set an intention to engage in an active imagination exercise.

• Sit with pen and paper, or at a computer, and invite a voice, image, or energy from your unconscious to make itself known. Wait to see what wants to emerge. Open yourself to whatever is there, and remember to "catch the tail" of any fleeting words, thoughts, or impressions that pop into your mind.

• If an image appears, whether familiar or unfamiliar, begin a dialogue by simply asking, "Who are you? Why have you come to me?" Then engage in conversation in whatever way feels appropriate. Depending on what appears—say, that giant orange parrot—it might not feel "appropriate" at all and may in fact feel bizarrely unfamiliar. Give yourself the freedom to get curious and explore without imposing conventional constraints on the experience. Remember, this is your imagination at work. Don't worry about what the neighbors will think; they'll never know unless you choose to tell them.

• If no image appears, keep in mind that this state of pure receptivity does not come naturally to many people. If this is the case, try one of the techniques below to facilitate the process. The techniques are deliberate methods for beginning the process, but remember that once begun, you'll need to let go of the reins and allow things to unfold organically. Active imagination doesn't work if you impose a map on it; it only works if you allow images and information to emerge freely from your unconscious (though you're free to stop it at any time).

  — Choose an image from a recurring fantasy, such as an idealized child or lover, or an animal that captivates your attention. You can also choose a person who has died with whom you wish to connect, as I did in the "Conversations with My Father" chapter of my memoir.

— Choose a figure that has appeared in a dream, perhaps one that you found particularly intriguing or offensive. Either way, the figure clearly carries a lot of energy for you. Hold the intent to reenter the dream and see what wants to happen next.

— Go to a safe place in your imagination, perhaps a beach, forest, private garden, or special room. Wait there for an image to appear.

— Identify a feeling or mood, and ask for an image to appear of who is feeling that way. (This is discussed further in the Subpersonalities section of this book.)

• Once you have an image to work with, allow a dialogue to unfold by letting your imagination lead the way. Ask the image why it has come to you and what it wants you to know. Adopt a welcoming stance as much as possible, letting the image know you're willing to listen to what it has to say. Feel free to say no to any activity that feels wrong to you, but as much as possible, discuss with the image why you don't want to participate. Include your feelings as well as your thoughts in the dialogue.

• As the dialogue unfolds, write down everything that happens and every verbal exchange. In addition to being able to refer to it later, keeping a written record helps you stay focused on the process and can prevent your mind from wandering. If you take to the process naturally and find that you stay focused with ease, you may prefer to speak and record everything that happens and transcribe the recording later.

• The dialogue is a give-and-take between your conscious self and your unconscious. While it's important to allow images to express themselves, it's unwise to give them free rein to run your life. If, for example, an image asks you to abandon all your responsibilities, you must bring your values to bear on your response. Again, you can and should say no to anything that feels wrong to you, but be sure to use this opportunity to get to know the part of you that wants to abandon all responsibilities. If it lives in your unconscious, it's probably already been impacting some aspect of your life, possibly through sabotage. By developing a relationship with it, you'll make it more conscious and find ways to balance its desires with the rest of you. (This topic is discussed in greater depth in the Observer Self and Subpersonalities sections of this book.)

• Ideally, it's best to stay with the image until a resolution takes place. The image emerged from your unconscious, and there's a reason it did. It wants to help you see or understand something that represents a next step in your growth. If you can't stay with the image because the experience is too intense, make an agreement to revisit the image after you've had time to assimilate what has happened. The process might require a series of active imagination sessions to resolve. In some cases, you might develop a relationship with an image over the course of months or even years.

• When a resolution has taken place and your active imagination experience is complete, create a concrete expression of it. This might be a ritual, a drawing or collage, or whatever feels appropriate—but definitely something that involves your emotions and your body. This activity will ground the experience in your cells and connect the symbols in your unconscious with your everyday life, which will facilitate integration of the experience.

The Observer Self

The observer self is an aspect of the psyche that can step back from everyday life and observe from a larger vantage point. You might consider it your inner wisdom or a wise aspect of yourself that you're able to access in calm, clear moments. Your observer self is connected to your core self, which can be likened to the hub of the wheel of your personality. While your moods and behaviors vary, the observer self operates from a perspective that can help make sense of it all, and even more, can help you integrate these diverse aspects. The observer self is an invaluable ally in personal growth and healing that you can "turn up the volume" on over time.

Try This: Contact Your Observer Self

• Find a quiet space and time away from your everyday routine. Arrange to be free of interruption by family members, pets, and the telephone.

• Close your eyes and take several deep breaths to calm yourself. Notice the feeling of the breath as it enters your body and fills you, and again as it leaves your body. Repeat this several times as you continue to notice the sensations that accompany your breathing.

• Notice any other sensations you may feel in your body—tension, relaxation, comfort or discomfort, hot or cold. Don't try to change the sensations; simply notice them.

• Direct your attention to any sounds you may hear around you—birds singing, the refrigerator humming, traffic whooshing by outside. Whatever you hear, just notice it. Notice how directing your attention to the outside sounds diminishes your awareness of the sensations in your body. Notice that you can shift your focus back and forth between internal sensations and external sounds.

- Now direct your attention to your feelings. Notice how you're feeling in this moment—happy, sad, angry, calm, agitated, or another emotion. Again, don't try to change the feelings; simply notice them. Notice also that when you tune in to your emotions, your awareness of sounds diminishes.

- Next, direct your attention to your thoughts. Notice the thoughts that are present in your awareness when you ask yourself, "What am I thinking right now?" Again, just notice what's there without trying to change anything.

- Review briefly your experience of directing your awareness, in turn, to your breath, other body sensations, the sounds in your environment, your feelings, and your thoughts. Imagine your attention as a spotlight you can aim at will in any of these directions. Review once again the places where you directed your awareness as you imagine shining a spotlight on each of them.

- Now ask yourself, "Who is aware? Who is this being who directs awareness? Who is this being who is outside of, yet aware of, all these experiences?"

This is your observer self, who is capable of identifying with or disidentifying from any experience you're having. When you have access to your observer self, you can strengthen the ability to step outside of any mood, feeling, or urge that surfaces and discover a greater power to direct your life instead of being at the effect of impulses that seem to overtake you. Your observer self can also help you learn about those impulses and listen with compassion and clarity to their wisdom and the messages they have for you. (The observer self is discussed further in the next section.)

Subpersonalities (Parts)

Subpersonalities are aspects within each of us that have their own distinct thoughts and feelings. (Subpersonalities may also be referred to as parts, aspects, ego states, and fragments in the psychological literature.) Some subpersonalities can be considered different "hats" we wear in various aspects of our lives: as spouse, parent, employee, or hobbyist. More extreme subpersonalities may have been created as a result of wounding (including, but not limited to, abuse and other trauma) and sometimes hold thoughts and emotions that "go underground," splitting off from the core of our personality because staying connected to them during painful moments was too difficult. It is not necessary to have a history of abuse or other trauma to benefit from working with these parts of us.

Subpersonalities are normal aspects of all of us, although the internal cast of characters varies from person to person. We may have aspects that embody the intellectual, taskmaster, adventurer, magical child, hermit, lover, competitor, topdog, underdog, and so on. Some subpersonalities are archetypal; that is, they embody blueprints of universal energies. Other subpersonalities are idealized images of oneself, such as Brad Pitt, Jennifer Lopez, Don Juan, or Mother Teresa. These idealized subpersonalities often appear in adolescence as young people try on various adult energies. Still other subpersonalities represent specific functions or aspects of self, such as thinking, feeling, and self-protection.

For various reasons, each of us has certain aspects that become unconscious, or "go underground." They can sabotage growth and can also wreak havoc on our lives. Like a child who wants attention but is repeatedly ignored or turned away, disowned subpersonalities can grow increasingly insistent on being heard and may have unique ways of throwing temper tantrums. For example, a healthy need for a break from responsibilities, if denied, can manifest in a serious illness that mandates rest or an impulsive trip right before a critical work deadline. An ignored subpersonality can also spark rage attacks and even outbursts of violence.

Disowned subpersonalities may seem to disappear completely, when in reality they are dormant or in hiding. This kind of disconnection from a subpersonality tends to limit a person's life in some way. For example, a healthy need for emotional expression, if denied, can develop over time into a complete lack of authentic emotion or, in some cases, contempt for authentic emotion. A healthy need for sexual expression, if denied, can cause myriad forms of internal disconnection that can range from completely rejecting the body to becoming a sexual abuser. This is seen in religious zealots who preach abstinence while acting out as pedophiles.

Identifying our subpersonalities and developing relationships with them can be a rich way to expand self-awareness; decode seemingly weird impulses, behaviors, and symptoms; and bring us into greater alignment with our core self. Over time, we can learn what triggers each of them and what needs each one is trying to express. We can learn to welcome them as helpful reminders of the need to slow down, find our voice, heal a past trauma, bring more beauty into our life, integrate a hidden need, or respond to other messages they may carry.

As you explore your subpersonalities, keep in mind that you're in charge. Neglected subpersonalities can get stubborn and militant if they've been ignored for a long time. It's important to listen to their essential message, but you are the final authority—they don't get to run the show. And the more you develop relationships with them over time, the less they *will* run the show. (See the Internal Family Systems and other listings at the back of the book for additional resources for working with subpersonalities.)

Try This: Discover Your Subpersonalities
(Adapted with permission from *What We May Be*, by Piero Ferrucci, pp. 48–49)

- Find a quiet space and time away from your everyday routine. Arrange to be free of interruption for this exercise.

- Reflect on a prominent trait, quality, or attitude of yours. You might choose the first one that comes to mind.

- Close your eyes and focus your attention on this aspect of yourself. Allow an image to spontaneously emerge that represents this aspect of you. It could be a human form (adult or child), an animal, a plant, a make-believe being, a rock, a car, or anything else in the entire world. Don't intentionally choose an image; rather, allow an image to reveal itself to you. Whatever comes is the right thing.

- When the image appears, be aware of it without interference or judgment. If interference or judgment is present to such a degree that you can't separate from it, make that the focus of this exercise.

- If the image changes or moves as you focus on it, just continue to observe it and allow it to show itself to you. Then become aware of the general feeling or energy of the image.

- Allow the image to communicate with you in whatever way it wishes. Regardless of whether it appears as animate or inanimate, it can communicate. Ask what it needs and what it wants you to know, and simply give it space to answer. This image you are observing and listening to is a subpersonality. It has a life of its own—its own feelings, needs, and motives.

- Open your eyes and write down everything that has taken place during this exercise. When you have finished, give the subpersonality any name that will help you remember and identify it later on, such as Nicey Nice, the Bully, Igor the Monster, Gimme, the Cynic, the Whiner, and so on. After you've named it, record everything you know about its personality, traits, preferences, and anything else it has shared with you. Take as much time as you need to learn all you can about this subpersonality.

- When you are finished, or at a different time, revisit this subpersonality to see if there's more to learn from it.

- At a different time, get acquainted with a different subpersonality by repeating the steps above. If you wish, you can again reflect on a prominent trait, quality, or attitude you hold. Another method for identifying a subpersonality is to recall a time when you behaved in a way that you consider atypical. Perhaps you later said something like, "I just wasn't myself" or "I don't know what came over me. That's not at all like me." Who was that? Give it room to step forward into your awareness, and gently begin to get acquainted with it.

Try This: Work with Your Subpersonalities
- *Identification/Disidentification*—Choose one of your subpersonalities (I'll use Nicey Nice as an example) and recall a time when it seemed to be "running the show." Remember how it feels to be filled with Nicey Nice's energy. Feel that energy in your body. Walk around the room as Nicey Nice. Give yourself some lines as if you're playing a part in a movie, such as "Whatever you want is fine with me" or "I'm not angry. I don't believe in being angry." Now shake off that energy and step back into your observer self. Reflect on the fact that sometimes the energy of that subpersonality overtakes you. Reflect on the fact that you can step outside of it. Write about what you just experienced.

- *Observer Self Conversation/Dialogue*—Have a conversation between your observer self and a subpersonality, either aloud or as a written dialogue. If you notice the conversation becoming tense or heated, explore the possibility that a second subpersonality joined the conversation. You can expand the conversation to include this new subpersonality.

- *Conversations Between Subpersonalities*—Choose two of your subpersonalities who seem to have something to say to each other. You might choose two who are at odds with each other or two who could become allies. Allow them to dialogue. Notice the different emotions and bodily sensations when each one is speaking. Write about your experience.

- *Reluctant Subpersonalities*—If you encounter a hint of a subpersonality that is reluctant to talk or otherwise engage with you, give it the space it needs. If it's been neglected for a long time, it might not trust your intentions or might feel confronted and unsafe. The first step in getting to know it is simply being aware of it. The next step is to allow it to be however it is without trying to change it. Over time, as it sees that you're not going to attack it or force it to go away or change, it might decide to open up.

- *Obstinate Subpersonalities*—Explore the possibility of negotiating with an obstinate or otherwise difficult subpersonality. Each one is expressing a valid, even if distorted, need or concern. Try taking a step in the subpersonality's direction, and ask it, in turn, to take a step in your direction. Over time, an initial compromise can lead to further common ground.

ART THERAPY

Art therapy is a powerful tool for engaging with the unconscious and bringing aspects of self into awareness. As discussed earlier, art therapy has nothing to do with artistic talent—it's simply a way to give voice to inner symbols. You may feel an impulse to create literal representations of people, houses, and other things in your life. Or you might draw energetic, symbolic, or scribbly representations of those things—or even images whose meanings elude you completely. Release the notion that either literal or symbolic is the "right" way to draw. Trust that the perfect images that "want out" will emerge; get out of the way and allow your inner self to express itself. Give yourself time to develop fluency with this medium of expression. Much like learning a foreign language, getting comfortable with accessing inner symbols may take time.

In order to give yourself to the art process, it's important to let go of ideas or plans about what you want to create or what it might mean. The goal of this work is listening and responding to impulses and intuitions using art materials. You might also have some cognitive understanding of what the artwork means. If you do, that's fine, but you can trust that even without the understanding, you're giving voice to a part of yourself by honoring your inner impulses. Over a period of weeks, months, or years, you might see themes develop.

Try This: Explore with Art
- Find a quiet space and time away from your everyday routine. Arrange to be free of interruption by family members, pets, and the telephone. Put on some mellow instrumental music or simply enjoy the silence.

- Sit with whatever art materials you feel prompted to use (see Materials discussion at the end of this section). I'll use drawing paper and oil pastels as an example for this exercise.

- Close your eyes and take several slow breaths, mentally releasing any thoughts you might have. Imagine for this period of time that your concerns have evaporated, and give yourself the gift of this time for yourself. As much as possible, also release ideas, plans, and expectations.

- Affirm your intention to listen to and honor whatever wisdom wants to emerge from your inner self. Be open to something completely unexpected showing up.

- If you feel so inclined, place your hands palms down on the paper, close your eyes, and ask the question, "What wants to emerge right now?" You may see an image in your mind, hear a word or phrase, or get a sensation of something that wants attention. If so, feel free to express it on paper or in another way that feels right to you. For example, if you feel an impulse to crumple a piece of paper and throw it at a wall, do it!

- If you don't receive an impression, ask yourself these questions and follow up with whatever action feels like the most immediate response to each question.
    — What color does my hand want to pick up?
    — What movement does my hand want to make?
    — What color next?
    — What wants to emerge?
    Allow yourself to get into a flow of attuning to the intuitive impulses you're feeling. Notice how "in the present" you feel when you attune in this way and how the rest of your life seems to drop away. This quality of presence is deeply nourishing. It's a natural stress reducer, and it's also a great way to bypass your inner critic or censor.

- Follow your impulses to create whatever image wants to come out. Take your time and continue to check in with yourself. Sense when the image is complete. There's no need to think about whether the page is filled. Empty spaces can be part of the process, too.

- If a part of your drawing feels particularly intriguing, surprising, or disturbing, you may want to try a technique called magnifying to explore it further. Use a new piece of paper to enlarge that section of your drawing, filling in details and other elements in whatever way your intuition prompts you. You may want to continue magnifying over a number of drawings or revisit the process over a series of days.

- If you have a sense of the meaning of your artwork, journaling can be a useful tool for exploring and recording the insights that come to you. If you don't have a sense of the meaning, you can still journal about how the experience felt, or try freewriting (see the section on Journaling). Even without knowing what your art "means," you still may notice that you felt nourished by the process. Perhaps it was the quiet time for yourself, or maybe it was the experience of expressing yourself with color and shapes instead of words. The images you drew might be part of a bigger process—perhaps a part of you needing attention that will emerge in greater fullness over time.

- If you are working with issues related to the body (embodiment, health, and so on), you might find it fruitful to get a large piece of butcher paper and have someone trace the outline of your body. Cut the paper long enough to leave extra room above and below your body in case you want to surround your body with colors, shapes, or words. Sit with the tracing until it speaks to you; then use art materials to fill in and/or surround the outline as you feel prompted. Take time to journal afterward.

• Remember that your art is for you; it's not for anyone else's eyes unless you want to share it. If you do, I recommend explaining beforehand that you prefer the other person to simply witness silently—to look at your art and listen to your experience with sensitivity. Because your images come from a deep place inside, other people's associations often aren't appropriate or useful.

Materials

You might enjoy experimenting with various media. Oil pastels (similar to crayons but with denser color) are among the easiest and cleanest to use. I sometimes use oil pastels for small drawings before bedtime because they're simple to use and clean up after. Chalk pastels are messier because they create chalk dust (a plastic tablecloth is recommended if you don't have an art room); however, their color is more easily blended and can be applied in many ways. I'm especially fond of applying them to my fingers and finger painting with them. I like the soft, subtle color blending I can achieve and the soft way I feel inside when I caress the colors. I also enjoy using chalk pastels to express passionate feelings, which are magnified by the vibrant colors and flying chalk dust.

You may want to experiment with other media, including clay, various kinds of paint (including face paint), mask making, and collage (including three-dimensional collage using a glue gun and found objects). You can also experiment with various kinds of paper. You may find that certain materials are best for particular moods. When I feel a need to release anger, I like black and red oil pastels on eighteen by twenty-four newsprint. When I feel an impulse to explore a kind of energy, such as the feminine, I often create a collage with magazine images (*National Geographic* is one of my favorites). When I feel restless and want to explore where I'm going—figuratively or literally—I often make a collage using a map as the base paper. Various materials offer different experiences of body involvement as well. If you feel prompted to involve your entire body, try a big chunk of clay or do some finger painting on a large piece of butcher paper.

Other Expressive Therapies

Art therapy falls under the umbrella of expressive arts therapies. This field also includes music therapy, dance/movement therapy, drama therapy, and more. If you feel drawn to these kinds of inner work, many resources exist for learning about them, including books, workshops, websites, and professional trainings.

Journaling

Journaling, like art, is a tool for accessing more of ourselves than we're consciously aware of in everyday life. It's a way to connect with the life energy that flows through each of us—the deeper person we each are at our core—as well as our many subpersonalities. Like art, journaling is an intentional act that over time strengthens our connection to our inner world. It's a way to get to know who we are beneath our conditioning—to step outside of the person we present to the world. Some people experience art or movement as their native language and use words as a secondary language. Others who feel more naturally connected to words may be particularly fond of journaling.

The more your everyday life speeds up from deadlines, crises, a drive to overachieve, or the frenzied pace of the modern world, the more you may find your intuitive side yearning for balance in the form of stillness. Journaling can be a way to find that stillness.

Journaling can be about discovering the place inside where feelings, choices, impulses, and motivations come from. It's a way to express inner aspects of your life, which over time may come together like a connect-the-dots exercise. Things get clearer as threads and themes emerge that have been percolating underground. This, in turn, can allow you to live a more conscious, intentional life and to reframe your outlook from a deeper perspective.

Some of the power of journaling is in the act of naming. You may feel in your body a sense of relief and resonance—an "aha"— when you've found the right words to describe a feeling or experience. You may know how affirming it feels to be deeply heard and understood by another person; journaling allows you to do that for yourself—to be your own best confidante. It's an act of self-witnessing, a way to affirm that your life is worthy of attention and respect. In truth, no one else has the capacity to love and honor you as fully as you can love and honor yourself because only you know what you truly need. And paradoxically, only by learning to love and honor yourself can you know that experience enough to fully receive it from others.

A journal can take the form of a blank book, a spiral-bound notebook, a computer, a roll of butcher paper, or anything else that feels right to you. You may even choose to speak into a recording device and transcribe your words later. Choosing the right journal and writing implement can be a creative act, a way of expressing your intention to honor your own tastes and desires. Some people enjoy using an artist's sketchbook and combining writing with art; portable art supplies such as colored pencils or a twelve-pack of oil pastels can be welcome adjuncts to the right pen or pencil.

Where and when you write are as personal as what you use to write. Journaling in the morning or before bedtime, at a neighborhood cafe, with your back against a tree, or in a different place on different days—it's completely up to you. Many people find it works best to be away from their daily routine and be free of family members, dirty dishes, and the perennial to-do list. Others only feel safe enough to delve into their deepest thoughts and feelings in the comfort of familiar, enclosed surroundings. There are no rules save one: do what feels right.

As with art, it's good to practice suspending judgment and asking your inner critic or censor to take a break. The more you can do this, the freer your inner self will feel to let out whatever wants out. You can go back later and extract meaning or, as with art, just let it cook and deliver insights in its own time.

Try This: Explore with Journaling

- *Freewrite*—Ask yourself a question, such as "What is my sadness/anger/fear about?" or "How do I feel about what just happened with my mother?" Then start writing and keep writing, nonstop, in a stream-of-consciousness style. Your writing will take you to places you didn't expect, and you're likely to learn some very interesting things about yourself.

- *Write with a Timer*—Set a timer for five or ten minutes and freewrite nonstop. If you run out of words, write your last sentence over again and again or write your first sentence again. Write what it's like for you when your mind is blank. Or if your mind is wandering, check out where it's leading you. Keep writing.

- *Start with a Phrase*—Choose a phrase, such as "I never knew," as a starting point for journaling. Write twenty sentences that start with the phrase. Here are a few of mine:
  — I never knew that I found myself when I was nine.
  — I never knew I had a penchant for anger.
  — I never knew that all good things are lost.
  — I never knew that before the rain, you can smell it coming.
  Other possible starting phrases include: I feel, I need, I hope, I believe, I fear, I love, I hate, I mourn, I am, I won't, and I will. Or make up your own based on what's inside that wants out.

- *Make a List*—One hundred things you're angry about, scared of, frustrated with, yearning for. One hundred wishes you have for your life. One hundred qualities you want to bring into your life. If you run out of things before you reach one hundred, ask yourself repeatedly, "And what else?" One hundred of anything will likely get to the heart of your thoughts and feelings.

- *Write a Letter to Someone Else*—As a journaling exercise, write a letter to someone who is deceased or someone with whom you have unfinished business (a parent, child, sibling, ex-partner, boss, and so on). Affirm before starting to write that you're under no obligation to share the letter with anyone; this exercise is specifically for giving voice to your feelings and thoughts. It's completely up to you whether you choose later to act on what you wrote in some way—there's no right or wrong.

• *Write a Letter to Yourself from Someone Else*—Write a letter to yourself from someone who is deceased or someone with whom you have unfinished business. Just see what comes.

• *Dialogue with Your Body or a Body Part*—This can be particularly fruitful if you are experiencing a physical challenge. Your body, or a particular part of your body, might hold some wisdom that you're ready to hear.

• *Write a Letter to Your Inner Critic*—If you have a particularly loud inner critic, write a letter to it or dialogue with it. When you have finished, reflect on where that critical voice came from.

• *Collect Quotations That Inspire You*—Collect quotations on any topic you'd like to think about more—grieving, living an authentic life, finding soul sustenance in nature, writers on writing—whatever feels right to you. Use the quotations as jumping-off points for freewriting.

• *Write for Ritual Release*—Write on a piece of paper something you're ready to release from your life—perhaps an old relationship, a bad habit, or a belief that no longer serves you. Place several large stones in the bottom of a Pyrex bowl, put the paper in the bowl, and set the paper on fire. As it burns, feel in your body the energy of that person, quality, or thing leaving your life. Feel the space that is now available for new possibilities.

Your unconscious is a rich world with unlimited resources for exploration, healing, and adventure. Nurturing a relationship with this part of you can reawaken natural knowing and support the development of a full, authentic life. It can also reveal a wellspring of wisdom and strength to help during times of difficulty and loss. May the tools in this book be as useful to you as they have been, and continue to be, to me.

Recommended Resources

Active Imagination

Hannah, Barbara. *Encounters with the Soul: Active Imagination as Developed by C.G. Jung.* Santa Monica, CA: Sigo Press, 1981.

Johnson, Robert. *Inner Work: Using Dreams & Active Imagination for Personal Growth.* San Francisco: Harper & Row, 1986.

Subpersonalities

Internal Family Systems Therapy:

Schwartz, Richard C. *Introduction to the Internal Family Systems Model.* Oak Park, IL: Trailheads Publications, 2001.

————. *You Are the One You've Been Waiting For: Bringing Courageous Love to Intimate Relationships.* Oak Park, IL: Trailheads Publications, 2008.

The Center for Self Leadership (the official IFS organization)
http://www.selfleadership.org
In-person and telephone practitioners, workshops, trainings, conferences, books, and other resources

Earley, Jay. *Self-Therapy: A Step-By-Step Guide to Creating Wholeness and Healing Your Inner Child Using IFS.* Larkspur, CA: Pattern System Books, 2012.

Earley, Jay, & Bonnie Weiss. *Freedom From Your Inner Critic: A Self-Therapy Approach.* Boulder, CO: Sounds True, 2013.

IFS Growth Programs
http://personal-growth-programs.com
IFS books, demo sessions, guided meditations, webinars, and courses for both therapists and the general public

Other subpersonalities resources:

Brown, Molly Young. *Growing Whole: Self-Realization on an Endangered Planet.* Mt. Shasta, CA: Psychosynthesis Press, 2009.

Ferrucci, Piero. *What We May Be: Techniques for Psychological and Spiritual Growth Through Psychosynthesis.* New York: Jeremy P. Tarcher, 1982.

Firman, John, & Ann Gila. *Psychosynthesis: A Psychology of the Spirit.* Albany, NY: State University of New York Press, 2002.

Stone, Hal, & Sidra Stone. *Embracing Our Selves: The Voice Dialogue Manual.* San Rafael, CA: New World Library, 1998.

Art Therapy and Process Art

Capacchione, Lucia. *The Art of Emotional Healing.* Boston: Shambhala Publications, Inc., 2001.

———. *The Creative Journal: The Art of Finding Yourself.* North Hollywood, CA: Newcastle Publishing Co., Inc., 1989.

———. *Recovery of Your Inner Child: The Highly Acclaimed Method for Liberating Your Inner Self.* New York: Simon & Schuster, 1991.

Cassou, Michele, & Stewart Cubley. *Life, Paint and Passion: Reclaiming the Magic of Spontaneous Expression.* New York: Jeremy P. Tarcher, 1995.

Diaz, Adriana. *Freeing the Creative Spirit: Drawing on the Power of Art to Tap the Magic and Wisdom Within.* San Francisco: Harper SanFrancisco, 1992.

Ganim, Barbara, & Susan Fox. *Visual Journaling: Going Deeper Than Words.* Wheaton, IL: Quest Books, 1999.

Malchiodi, Cathy A. *The Art Therapy Sourcebook.* Los Angeles: Lowell House, 1998.

————. *The Soul's Palette: Drawing on Art's Transformative Powers for Health and Well-Being.* Boston: Shambhala Publications, Inc., 2002.

Williams, Heather. *Drawing as a Sacred Activity: Simple Steps to Explore Your Feelings and Heal Your Consciousness.* Novato, CA: New World Library, 2002.

The Painting Experience
http://www.processarts.com
Process art workshops, retreats, study groups, and individual mentoring

Journaling

Berg, Elizabeth. *Escaping into the Open: The Art of Writing True.* New York: HarperCollins Publishers, Inc., 1999.

DeSalvo, Louise. *Writing as a Way of Healing: How Telling Our Stories Transforms Our Lives.* San Francisco: HarperSanFrancisco, 1999.

Jacobs, Beth. *Writing for Emotional Balance: A Guided Journal to Help You Manage Overwhelming Emotions.* Oakland, CA: New Harbinger Publications, 2005.

Johnson, Alexandra. *Leaving a Trace: On Keeping a Journal: The Art of Transforming a Life into Stories.* Boston: Little, Brown and Company, 2001.

Acknowledgments

Deep gratitude is extended to:

My father, Lou Silverberg, whose modeling and encouragement helped me learn to live true to myself and whose passing sparked the emergence of my writer-self;

Nina Menrath, for introducing me to art therapy and parts work at a 1989 Findhorn Foundation workshop and providing me with a wealth of tools for getting to know myself at a deeper level;

Dick Schwartz, for developing the Internal Family Systems Model, which has been instrumental in my healing since 2007, and to IFS trainers Toni Herbine-Blank, Chris Mathna, Kay Gardner, Susan McConnell, and Paul Ginter for support and insights;

My husband, Charlie—you know, Beloved.

About the Author

KIRA FREED, MA, LPC, BCC, is a licensed mental health counselor, certified life and wellness coach, and freelance writer who holds two master's degrees, one in integral counseling psychology from the California Institute of Integral Studies and the other in anthropology from the University of Colorado–Boulder. She also holds a certificate in nonfiction writing from the University of Washington–Seattle and has completed Levels 1–3 professional trainings in the Internal Family Systems Model.

In addition to doing therapy with individuals and couples, Kira has cofacilitated women's self-discovery groups that combine expressive arts, journaling, and guided imagery. Her current human development work is a blend of life and wellness coaching with the Internal Family Systems Model.

Kira has written more than 175 books for educational publishers, including Learning A–Z, Benchmark Education, Wright Group/McGraw-Hill, Rosen Publishing, and Zaner-Bloser. The books, written at graduated levels of complexity, are used to teach elementary schoolchildren to read while introducing them to high-interest content. Topics range from nonfiction subjects such as history, biography, and life science to a fictionalized third-grade adaptation of her memoir *Losing and Finding My Father* titled *Losing Grandpa*.

Kira lives in Tucson, Arizona, with her husband, Charlie Alolkoy, an artist. She can be reached at:

www.kirafreedcoaching.com
www.losingandfindingmyfather.com